better together*

*This book is best read together, grownup and kid.

 **akidsco.com**

a kids book about

IMAGINATION

by LeVar Burton

A Kids Co.
Editor Denise Morales Soto
Designer Duke Stebbins
Creative Director Rick DeLucco
Studio Manager Kenya Feldes
Sales Director Melanie Wilkins
Head of Books Jennifer Goldstein
CEO and Founder Jelani Memory

DK
Editor Emma Roberts
Senior Production Editor Jennifer Murray
Senior Production Controller Louise Minihane
Senior Acquisitions Editor Katy Flint
Managing Art Editor Vicky Short
Publishing Director Mark Searle

This American Edition, 2023
Published in the United States by DK Publishing
1745 Broadway, 20th Floor, New York, NY 10019

DK, a Division of Penguin Random House LLC

A catalog record for this book is available from the Library of Congress.
ISBN: 978-0-7440-8570-9

DK books are available at special discounts when purchased in bulk for
sales promotions, premiums, fund-raising, or educational use. For details, contact:
DK Publishing Special Markets, 1745 Broadway, 20th Floor, New York, NY 10019, or SpecialSales@dk.com

Printed and bound in China

For the curious
www.dk.com

akidsco.com

MIX
Paper | Supporting
responsible forestry
FSC™ C018179

This book was made with Forest
Stewardship Council™ certified
paper - one small step in DK's
commitment to a sustainable future.
**For more information go to
www.dk.com/our-green-pledge**

I dedicate this book to the dreamer
who lives in us all.

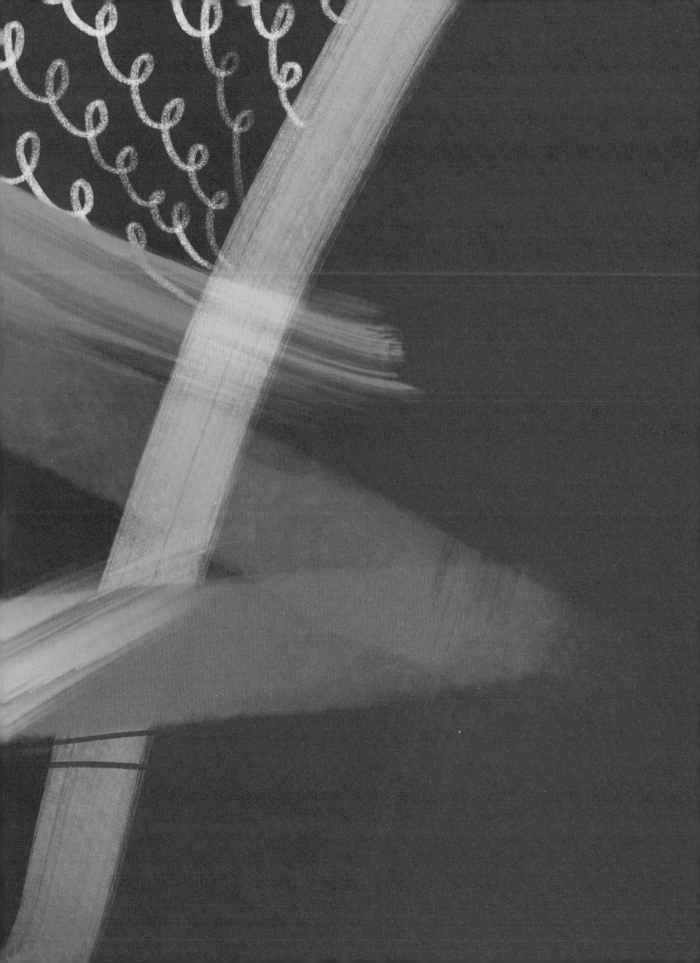

Intro
for grownups

It's critical we develop a healthy relationship with our imagination. The older we get, the less we tend to exercise that muscle. This is one of the reasons I wanted to write this book—to ignite curiosity, foster empathy, and promote a healthy exercising of our imagination from an early age.

This upcoming generation will inherit the problems and injustices the previous generations failed to solve. It will be incumbent upon them to solve these issues in the future, and chief among the tools they will need in order to do so is their imagination.

You see, our imagination is the most powerful thing we have. It allows us to visualize the possibility of "*what if?*".

So, as you read this book with your future changemaker, do yourself a favor and exercise your own imagination muscle—*imagine* the conversations you'll have after you've shared this together!

heroes.

How about you?

The reason I love superheroes is because they have the power to change the world and make it a better place.

But I've learned that you don't have to be a superhero to change the world.

In fact, I believe
every human being

has a superpower...

I know this because
I've been to the future
and I've been to the past.*

*Just ask your grownup, they might
know what I'm talking about.

I've lived countless lives through my many roles as an actor.

I've been enslaved on a plantation in Georgia in the 1860s.

I've explored the galaxy in a starship with an intrepid* crew.

I've read stories to millions of children all over the world.

*Intrepid means to be bold, brave, and adventurous.

All because of my imagination.

My name is LeVar and I'm an actor, writer, director, podcaster, and most importantly,

a story-teller.

And everywhere I go, I ask one question, using 2 of the most powerful words in the world: "What if?"

Asking "What if?"
is all about possibility...

What if frogs could fly?

What if homework was optional?

What if I could love and accept myself just the way I am?

When I ask "What if?",
I use my superpower,

imagi-
nation.

Imagination is the power
to dream up the world
the way you'd like it to be.

Thinking up not just what **is**,
but what **could be**.

I didn't find this superpower on my own.

My mother, Erma Gene,
was an avid reader.

She introduced me to
the world of books.

In books, I found companionship, adventure, magic, and inspiration.

Even though they are just filled with words, and sometimes pictures, books are also full of entire universes.

They helped me see the world as a place where I belonged.

They made me more

empow-
─ered.

They made me more

courag eous.

They also made me feel less alone.

Imagine all that, just from books!
But that's how imagination works.

Imagination is a tool for

change.

Imagination is the machine we use to

invent.

Imagination is our creativity in

action.

We can imagine ourselves in the past, present, and future, and no other species on earth can do that.

Now, you might think you

aren't any

god

at using your imagination.

But one of the best things about our imagination is that we are using it all the time, even if we aren't aware of it.

Have you ever thought about what or who you might be when you grow up?

Have you ever watched TV and pretended you were one of the characters?

Have you ever considered how things might have gone had you made a different decision about something?

You have?

Well, you've used your imagination!

Now, here's the important part:

imagination is a **muscle**.

While we're all born with it,
did you know you
can **strengthen** it?

Flex your
imagination by

UP

bigger and
brighter futures.

about everything.

Don't accept things as they are.

Think of how they COULD BE.

Tell stories how **you** wish to tell them, not simply the way they have been told to you.

Think of the possibilities when asking:

"What if?"

Imagination is SO important!

Everything made by people is the product of imagination.

Every great movement started with someone using their imagination.

Every great invention is created by someone using their imagination.

Every great problem is solved by someone using their imagination.

When we don't use our imagination...

we actually limit the possibilities that exist in our world.

Yes, you, the kid reading this book.

Your imagination is more powerful

than you think.

YOU are powerful.

So use your superpower
and imagine, "what if?"

What if you lived in a world that was fair for everyone?

What if prejudice or racism didn't exist?

What if everyone you cared about felt safe and loved?

What if every kid felt
like they belonged?

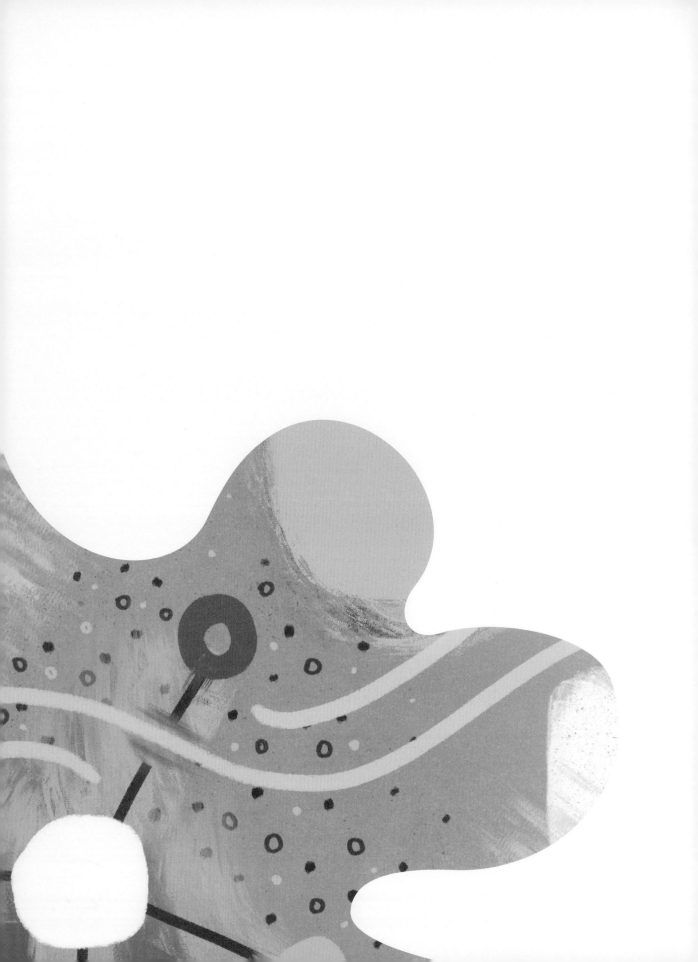

What if everyone, everywhere, had what they needed to survive?

What if the future holds something incredible for you?

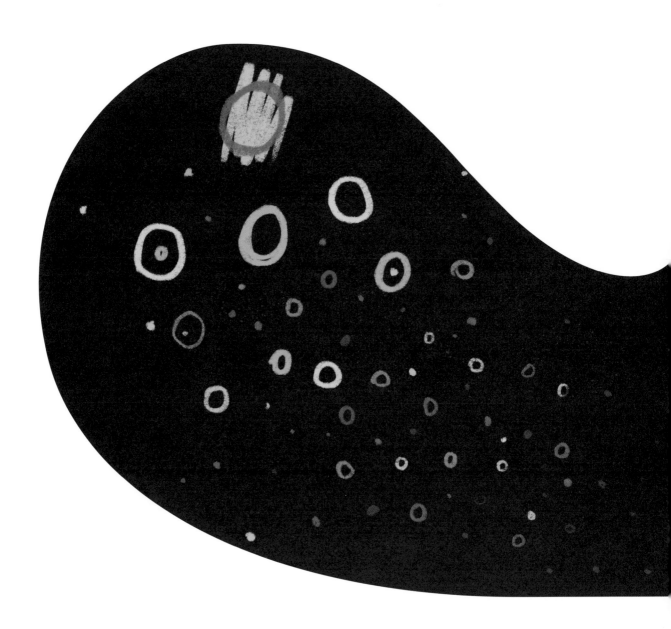

Just imagine...

what if?

Outro
for grownups

Now that you and your kid have unlocked your innate superpower and flexed your imagination muscles, my hope is that you will actively engage in the development and strengthening of both—today, tomorrow and for your kid, well into their adult life.

Encourage them to never stop asking, "What if?" And when they do, don't be afraid to engage in the process along with them.

Our imagination reinforces possibility as great as the universe—and that's endless.

But you don't have to take my word for it.

About The Author

LeVar Burton (he/him) has dedicated his life to the power of storytelling—a privilege he does not take lightly.

As the son of an English teacher, Burton's introduction to reading was early, and consuming. Inside the pages of good books, he harnessed his imagination and found himself transported to other worlds, enjoying casts of characters he counts among friends to this day.

Throughout his career he's shared stories as an actor, writer, director, producer, public speaker, and podcaster. No matter the medium, it is his steadfast belief that stories have the ability to bring people together. Because when we engage with stories, we gain insight about ourselves, our world, and the importance of empathy for others.

 @levar.burton   @levarburton   🌐 levarburton.com

Made to empower.

a kids book about **racism**
by Jelani Memory

a kids book about ANXIETY
by Ross Szabo

a kids book about DISABILITY
by Kristine Napper

a kids book about IMAGINATION
by LEVAR BURTON

a kids book about belonging
by Kevin Carroll
Bestselling Author of
Rules of the Red Rubber Ball

a kids book about failure
by Dr. Laymon Hicks

a kids book about GRATITUDE
by Ben Kenyon

a kids book about LIFE ONLINE
by Dave S. Anderson
& Blake Fleischacker

a kids book about body image
by Rebecca Alexander

a kids book about IMMIGRATION
by MJ Calderon

a kids book about EMPATHY
by Daron K. Roberts

a kids book about GENDER
by Dale Mueller